Maria Elisa Avagnina

The Teatro Olimpico

photographs by Pino Guidolotti

Guide Marsilio

Thanks to Franco Barbieri
and Guido Beltramini
for their valuable suggestions

cover
Row of statues seen from the right
partition window
photograph by Pino Guidolotti

Layout
Tapiro, Venice

© 2005 by Marsilio Editori® s.p.a.
in Venezia
ISBN 978-88-317-8731-4

www.marsilioeditori.it

Contents

7 The Accademia Olimpica commissioner
of the theatre: a 'select company of virtuous
and noble spirits'

10 The new theatre premises: 'in the courtyard
of the old prison' at the *Isola*

13 A dazzling design, a moving testament

15 An 'ancient' but modern theatre:
Vitruvius' lesson and Palladio's invention

19 Problems of authorship: the Palladio theatre
and Vincenzo Scamozzi's perspectives

24 Theatre space as place of illusion

29 The statues in the Palladio hall: 'casting the
academician founders of the theatre in stone'
and the question of 'everlasting memory'

36 The reliefs with *Episodes from the Life
of Heracles*: a chapter of humanist culture
in euhemeristic vein

40 'Anno MDLXXXIIII Palladio archit[ecto]', a
stone and a statue: recognition, but late and
lacking sincerity

42 *Alla ducale* and 'false air' ceiling, or single
curtain? The terms of a raging debate

43 The theatre and its tragedy: the opening
performance of Sophocles' *Oedipus the King*

45 Vestibule and odeum

HOC OPVS HIC LABOR EST

VIRTVTI AC GENIO
OLYMPICOR ACADEMIA THEATRVM HOC
A FVNDAMENTIS EREXIT
ANN MDLXXXIIII PALLADIO ARCHIT.

previous pages:
1. The proscenium
and scenery perspectives

2. The Accademia emblem
conceived by Elio Belli
in 1556 in the upper tier
of the proscenium; below,
the dedicatory inscription

The Accademia Olimpica commissioner of the theatre: a 'select company of virtuous and noble spirits'

The Teatro Olimpico, the first permanent covered theatre of the Renaissance, was not the expression of a royal court, a powerful seigniory or an enlightened municipality, but of a private noble group with cultural aims.

Miraculously preserved entirely in its original appearance, it arose out of the will of the Olimpico academicians, who sponsored its construction to a design by Andrea Palladio between 1580 and 1585. In order to fully appreciate the singularity and essence of this extraordinary creation, it is therefore necessary to briefly retrace the history of its commissioning body.

The Accademia Olimpica, still in existence and widely active, was formed in 1555 by 21 founding members, including Palladio himself, in the atmosphere of cultural openness and ferment that marked the years immediately preceding the conclusion of the Council of Trent (1563). Other academies also appeared in Vicenza in those same years, such as that of the *Secreti* and that of the *Costanti*, the latter being extremely conservative and of strictly religious orthodoxy.

The Accademia Olimpica was distinguished at its foundation among contemporary intellectual guilds not only by its declared commitment to scientific disciplines, but also by its more open and democratic social composition. Its membership consisted not only of members of the established nobility and aristocracy of wealth, but also of exponents of the professions and arts.

The cultural, particularly scientific, aims set by the members to be pursued through application and study were evident right from the introduction to the first academic *Statuti*. This dates from 1 March 1556 and proudly states that every member 'desires to learn all the sciences and especially mathematics, which is the true decoration of all who possess a noble and virtuous spirit'.

The interest in physics, astronomy and anatomy also emerges from the inventory of papers and properties owned by the Accademia, unfortunately now lost. They included astrolabes, metal and wooden spheres, globes, maps, wax and terracotta figures, 'casts of all the parts of man', including 'two legs of Christ by Michiel Angelo' and 'the thigh of Laocoon'.

The aspirations and intellectual commitment of the society at the time of its constitution are effectively expressed by the motto adopted by the founder members, and by the choice of Heracles as its tutelary deity, whose name evokes the pan-Hellenic Olympic games, founded in honour of the demigod.

The motto, conceived in 1556 by the academician Elio Belli, an eminent and renowned doctor and physicist, is engraved in characters at the top of the proscenium and, in its original version, later abbreviated, reads: HOC OPUS HIC LABOR EST (fig. 2). Taken from a passage in Virgil's *Aenead*, it alludes to the difficulty those who descend to the underworld have in ascending from the shadows of Avernus to the light of the sun; a metaphor for the difficulty of reaching the light of truth and knowledge by way of darkness.

Similarly, Heracles, conceived out of the love of Alcmene and Zeus, lord of the gods, who attained the divine prerogative of immortality by accomplishing superhuman tests, the mythical 'twelve labours', was taken up by the Olympians as a symbol of the strength and suffering needed to achieve knowledge and with it the immortality of glory and fame.

The concept is made clear at a figurative level by the damaged statue of the hero now in the south-east corner of the odeum (fig. 32) and the splendid bas-reliefs on the proscenium depicting *Stories from the Life of Heracles*. There is then also the frontispiece of the Accademia's *Statuti* of 1650 engraved by Giacomo Ruffoni, who in a single image depicted the tutelary deity and the Olympic motto in the shortened form HOC OPUS (fig. 3).

Imbued with Aristotelian thinking, the members intended replacing a static, dogmatic view of knowledge with a secular, empirical, dynamic one based on constant research, as seems suggested by the relentless rush of chariots in the stadium shown in the background of the emblem.

3. Giacomo Ruffoni, frontispiece of the *Statuti dell'Accademia Olimpica*, etching, c. 1650

Alongside the exact and natural sciences, the Olympians professed a fervent interest in theatre right from the start, expressed through the production of plays. These included the renowned *L'amor costante* by Alessandro Piccolomini and *Sofonisba* by Giangiorgio Trissino, respectively performed during the carnival celebrations of 1561 and 1562. They were staged in the main hall of the Basilica, in a temporary, wooden theatre especially built by Palladio inside the big gothic space.

The idea of building a permanent theatre dates from the early 1580s, and the academicians once again turned to their famous architect colleague to design it.

Construction of the theatre, which was officially opened on 3 March 1585 with the staging of *Oedipus Rex* by Sophocles, marked an important stage in the history of the Accademia and created the basis of its undying fame, inseparably linked to that Palladio masterpiece and destined to continue well beyond the end of the century.

The exciting but turbulent theatre project was completed mainly because of the decisive involvement of Leonardo Valmarana, the *principe* in office from January 1583 to 1585. But at the turn of the sixteenth century, the original drive and secular openness of the Accademia, which had already weakened in the preceding years, went into decline as a result of the heavy ideological restrictions exerted by the Counter Reformation. An aristocratic and oligarchic stiffening took place in the ranks of the Olympians, moving the

4-5. Two frescoed scenes
in vestibule: *Diplomatic mission
of Japanese envoys; Tournament*

Accademia away from the more liberal and democratic dialectic of its beginnings. The main proponent of this was Pompeo Trissino, grandson of the great Giangiorgio and member of the oldest and most illustrious Vicentine aristocracy. He was repeatedly elected *principe* of the society in those years and was responsible for the group's new *Statuti* (1596) and for completion of the vestibule and construction of the odeum (1608-9) next to the theatre.

At the same time, overt pro-imperial propensities were becoming established among the more authoritative members of the association, though this was nothing new to the Vicentine nobility. Attitudes of opposition to Venetian rule were also appearing, and these were probably the reason the Venetian *podestà*, Benedetto Zorzi, was intentionally absent from the inaugural performance.

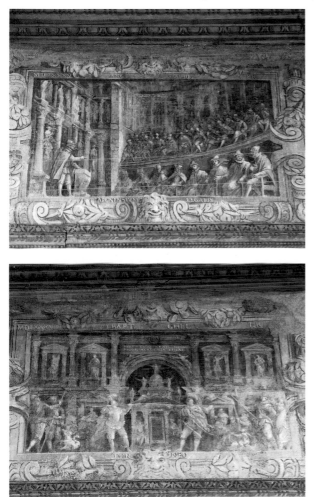

In the seventeenth century the Olimpico gradually developed a ceremonial role, which eventually replaced its original theatre function: from a place of theatrical performance it became one of entertainment. It became a formal, exclusive space in which the academicians saw themselves proudly reflected, and a point of reference for big civic and international events, such as the visit of the Japanese diplomatic mission in 1585, documented by one of the frescoed monochromes in the vestibule (fig. 4).

Apart from the presentation of Torquato Tasso's *Torrismondo*, successfully staged in 1618, the chronicles of the Accademia do not refer to any significant theatre or cultural initiatives in those decades, but there are frequent mentions of sumptuous receptions offered to illustrious guests, with 'well-prepared lamps' and musical accompaniment.

In a markedly sophisticated atmosphere and a context of increasing violence and unrest in Vicenza, the academicians, heedless of the scientific interests of the past, made urgent requests to their *principe* for a fencing teacher so that tournaments and barriers could be set up in the theatre, as shown in some of the other frescoed pictures in the vestibule (fig. 5).

Only towards the middle of the eighteenth century did the cultural interests at the heart of the Accademia seem to find renewed vigour, with a chair of experimental philosophy being established in 1741 and a debate revived on the sciences and art.

In 1755, stimulated by one of the recurring projects to restore the theatre's ceiling, a heated controversy flared up about its original roof, as designed by Palladio. This began in the Accademia but quickly went beyond the confines of Vicenza, being taken up by the most eminent architectural critics of the time, and continuing through to the new century.

Then, on 19 January 1813, no longer able to support the cost of its theatre, the Accademia ceded it to the Vicenza city administration, which had originally provided the land for its construction almost two and a half centuries before. But the Accademia retained the right to continue holding its own academic sessions in the building and to stage a cycle of classical plays annually.

The new theatre premises: 'in the courtyard of the old prison' at the *Isola*

The 'almost constant silence' following the staging of Trissino's *Sofonisba* in 1562 persuaded the members to enthusiastically reinstate the idea of theatre performances at the sitting of 10 August 1579. Then, on 15 February 1580, wanting to resume the interrupted tradition and with the aim of building a permanent theatre for the performances, the academicians decided, on the initiative of the newly elected *principe*, Pietro Porto, to present the *Magnifica Comunità di Vicenza* with a request for a suitable venue, identified as a covered area in the old city prison.

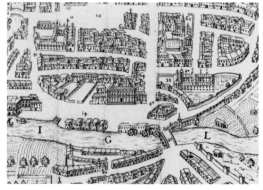

6. Giacomo Monticolo, *Urbis Vicentiae*, 1611, detail with the Piazza dell'Isola (14) and the Castello del Territorio (47). Vicenza, Biblioteca Civica Bertoliana, R.I.V. Cart. C.18

The procedure was very rapid and crowned with success: on 22 February the request was presented to the city representatives; it underwent some alterations on the twenty-fourth and on the next day was approved by the Council of the 100.

The chosen area was within the confines of the old Castello di S. Pietro, later known as the 'Territorio' (fig. 6). This was a fortified building erected in the eastern part of the city in the thirteenth century to control the nearby bridge over the Bacchiglione and the road to Padua, along the eastern part of the Roman decumano – the current Corso Palladio – in front of the 'Piazza dell'Isola'.

The latter is the name that historically described the area between the Bacchiglione and Retrone rivers, which flow into one another a short distance away.

The fortified nature of the building is still apparent in the surviving Coxina tower (fig. 9) to the north and in the crenellated wall visible along the south-west side of the perimeter wall. The late fifteenth-century entrance in red stone, which originally provided access to the theatre, can still be seen here. It was later flanked, fur-

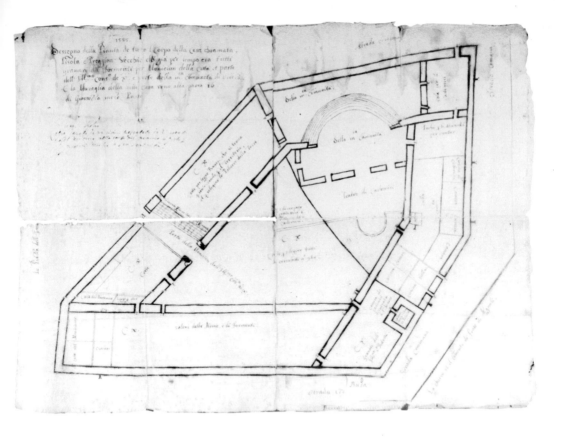

7. Anonymous, *Layout drawing of the entire building known as the Isola, Old Prison*, 1585, ink on paper, mm 436 x 575. Vicenza, Musei Civici D 52

ther north, by the ashlared doorway that opens onto the vestibule, built by Scamozzi (fig. 10).

The layout of the area at the time of the theatre's construction is faithfully shown by a contemporary drawing in the Vicenza Musei Civici, which is the first, reliable document concerning it (fig. 7). The drawing, dating from 1585, records masonry and wooden dividing structures inside the trapezoidal perimeter of the castle, no longer extant, which highlight the common nature of the court area, both in terms of ownership and use. The 'Corte del Theatro' on the west side, owned by the Magnifica Comunità but ceded in use to the Accademia, was flanked by a larger area on the east. This was owned by the Venetian government and entrusted to the office of the 'Territorio' to house stores of grain, arms and munitions.

The gate on the southern side of the complex, surmounted by the coat of arms of the Venetian captain Francesco Tiepolo, was opened up by Ottavio Bruti Revese in 1600 and provided access to the 'Corte del Territorio'. It has been used since the nineteenth century as the entrance to the theatre through the garden (fig. 9).

The isolated location and absence of any clear external evidence of the theatre are still its peculiar features, able to increase its charm by giving it the secret and exclusive character of a hidden wonder. It was not until the second half of the nineteenth century, on the occasion of the third centenary of Palladio's death (1880), that a competition to give the theatre a monumental facade was held by

8. The outside wall
of the Castello di San Pietro
seen from the south west

the city, prompted by the desire to bestow civic dignity and enno-
ble the site. Of all the sumptuous and grandiloquent designs presented, none was to be built, fortunately leaving the appearance of
the original complex and area unchanged.

In this area in late February 1580, after a decision of great signifi-
cance for the future, the Olympians set about building the first permanent theatre in modern history, giving a tangible response to
one of the most typical dreams of the early Renaissance courts.

A dazzling design, a moving testament

With the old town prison site having been obtained under a concession and the project entrusted by the Olympians to their 'co-
academician Palladio', works on the new theatre proceeded with
surprising speed.

The feverish pace with which he drew up the plan suggests a long-
term familiarity with the theatre idea and a consummate theoreti-
cal and practical maturity. Indeed, Palladio was 72 at the time and
at the peak of his career and fame. Palladio's theatre was inspired by
those of the classical world and he lifted its design from the archive
of his memory as if from a roomy drawer. It had been nurtured and
considered over the course of 40 years from the time of his first trip
to Rome in 1541. So he took on the opportunity of the job he had
been assigned with enthusiasm and operational lucidity, pursuing
it so tenaciously that it seemed almost an 'own commission'.

The completely original building emerged from the contrast
between the chosen classical model and the contingencies of the
site, and showed both his fidelity to the prototype and his clever
invention It is precisely this intelligent capacity for adaptation that
marks it as an unrepeatable masterpiece.

A single drawing, a precious incunabulum of Palladio's thinking,
survives from the conception stage of the theatre, held by the Royal Academy of British Architects of London (fig. 14).

Attributed by critics to Palladio himself, possibly with the assis-
tance of his son Marcantonio in the actual drawing, the sheet pres-
ents an advanced stage of the project and is convincingly identified
with the 'model' of the theatre mentioned by the Accademia
sources, on the basis of the two versions of the proscenium, of
which the slightly lower one on the right is very similar to its final
appearance.

But the rapid start to the works was brought to a sudden standstill
by Palladio's death, on 19 August 1580, less than six months after
work on the project began, depriving him of the satisfaction of see-
ing his great dream come true.

The cherished plan of the theatre, the last, indispensable step in the
dream of classical *renovatio* pursued by the Vicentine nobility of the
time and given form by Andrea di Pietro della Gondola, classically
re-baptised as Palladio, was thus transformed into a moving spiri-
tual testament, which concluded his successful career with a

theme that was central to Renaissance society and particularly dear to the architect himself.

With Palladio's direction missing from the site, it was only the strength and integrity of his planning idea that ensured construction stayed more or less faithful to the original design, despite the intervention and inevitable adaptations made after his death.

An 'ancient' but modern theatre: Vitruvius' lesson and Palladio's invention

In designing the permanent theatre for the Olympians, Palladio suggested building an 'antique' theatre modelled on those of classical traditions. Despite the narrow dimensions of the site obtained by concession, he proposed the layout of a Roman theatre as conjectured by Vitruvius, the first century BC Roman architect and essayist, in his *De Architectura*, and was supported in this by his academic colleagues who wished him to 'sit Vitruvius alter'.

In this choice, pursued with determination, Palladio revealed aspects of the education he had received within the cultural circle of Alvise Cornaro, Giangiorgio Trissino, his discoverer and first patron, and Daniele Barbaro – all leading exponents of Veneto humanism in the first half of the sixteenth century. Andrea had worked with Barbaro in particular on the edition of Vitruvius' *Ten Books* published in 1556. He had provided drawings for the volume and

9. The Torre Coxina seen from the Ottavio Bruti Revese entrance

10. Vincenzo Scamozzi, ashlared doorway

suggestions based on his direct experience of the Roman monuments, thus taking a critical part in the fervent debate on the antique theatre and its reconstruction. In the preceding decades this had seen the involvement, as much speculative as genuinely applicable, of people like Leon Battista Alberti, Raphael, Baldassarre Peruzzi, Antonio da Sangallo, Sebastiano Serlio and Daniele Barbaro.

Onto these premises he grafted the outcomes of the continuing research he had conducted for about 40 years, from 1541 to 1580, through surveys, drawings and new elaborations of the remains of classical theatres, from those of the Marcello Theatre in Rome, to those of the Roman theatres in Verona and Pula and, of course, the Berga theatre in Vicenza, at the time still partly standing and visible. As the final stage in an evolutionary process developed through the temporary theatres set up in the Vicenza Basilica in 1561 and 1562 and in the Palazzo Dolfin in Venice for the *Compagnia della Calza* in 1565, the Olimpico was the umpteenth, and for Palladio the most extreme, application of the classical ideal. It marks a solid and enduring arrival point in the long search for the 'modern theatre space'.

So, empowered by the perfectly assimilated classical lesson, but constrained by practical demands, Palladio dropped his theatre into the existing walled box of the old city prison. His design solution made a rigorous and innovative interpretation of the chosen plan, used as a proportional reference for sizing the various parts of the building.

He translated the circular matrix of the model into an elliptical shape because of the narrowness of the space, but stayed within the bounds of Vitruvius' geometrical layout, based on four equilateral triangles in a circumference (fig. 11), as Ottavio Bertotti Scamozzi, that acute interpreter of Palladio's architecture, clearly highlighted in his drawings of the Olimpico (fig. 12) in 1776.

This is the reason behind the unusual oval shape of the audience hall (*cavea*) and its steep slope, pitched down toward the orchestra pit, and for the dynamic tension of the peristyle ending it above. This is in turn contained by the old castle wall, tangential to the curve of the colonnade.

The layout is also the reason for the greater longitudinal expansion of the proscenium (*scaenae frons*), which at the Olimpico reaches 25 metres, and the permanent connection of this to the partition walls (*versurae*) that define the stage (*proscenio*) on the short sides; such elements are not normally structurally connected in Roman theatres. Finally, the deepening of the orchestra pit is related, as an indirect consequence; it was originally lower, as if sunk into a spatial funnel, prior to the alterations made in the eighteenth and mid-twentieth centuries.

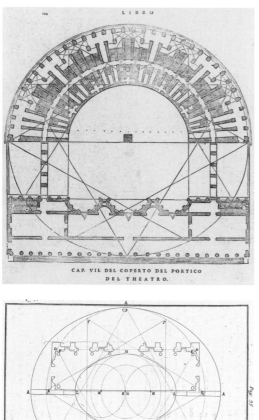

11. *Plan of Roman theatre*, from Vitruvius, *De Architectura*, V, 6, edited by Daniele Barbaro, 1556

12. Ottavio Bertotti Scamozzi, *Vitruvian geometric plan applied to the layout of the Teatro Olimpico*, from *Le Fabbriche*, I, 1776

13. Outside of the theatre seen from the garden

Moving from the plan to the elevation, Palladio's recovery of the classical lesson is evident in the spatial arrangement of the proscenium, marked by three orders of columns (*columnatio*) and a busy set of statues on plinths, in niches and aedicules. More than a triumphal arch, from a semantic point of view this structure recalls the elevation of a 'noble building', a *palazzo* of some importance, facing onto a closed square consisting of the front part of the stage, evoking a glimpse of an urban scene.

The body of the Palladio theatre, obtained by adapting and completing the existing frame of the old prison with restricted new construction work, denotes a stringent integrity and compactness,

14. Andrea Palladio
(and assistants?), *Draft plan for
the Teatro Olimpico*, 1579-80
pen, ink and watercolour
on watermarked paper,
417 x 89 mm.
London, R.I.B.A., BD VIII, fol. 5

despite the spatial constraints and enforced re-use of existing structures, due to the consistent conceptual unity behind the design. This is highlighted by the striking view of the theatre space from behind the peristyle columns (figs. 15-17), repeating – not by chance – the original access way for the audience prior to the unfortunate opening up of the two rectangular doorways in the lower part of the cavea, dating from the mid-twentieth century. From this elevated position the view synthetically takes in the articulate co-penetration of spaces and linkages of levels and thoroughfares created by Palladio: it quickly descends the slope of the cavea, drops into the orchestra pit and ranges across the floor of the stage, to come suddenly up against the uneven wall of the proscenium or, moving to the side, to run along the columns of the exedra, led on by the reflection of light on the marmorino of their trunks.

The originality and modernity of Palladio's creative process will not escape the modern visitor, as it did not escape the visitor of his day: a kind of conceptive energy that was unleashed by the meeting of an

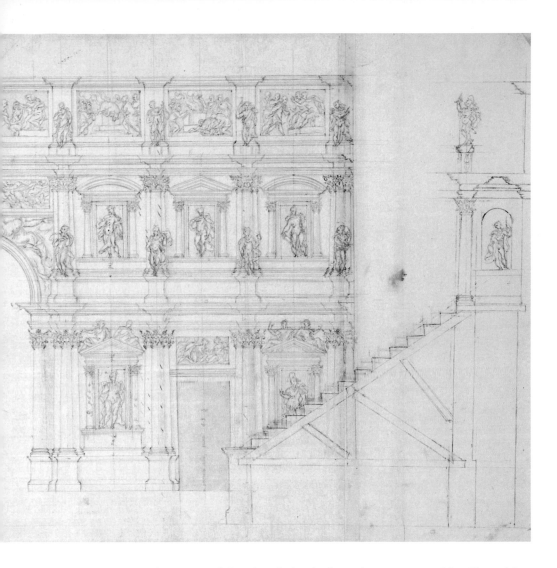

abstract model and real physical requirements, capable of breathing new life into the pages of the treatise and the ruins of history.

Problems of authorship: the Palladio theatre and Vincenzo Scamozzi's perspectives

While Palladio's authorship of the theatre itself has never been placed in doubt by scholars, confirmed mainly by the evidence of stylistic elements but also by the inscription on the front of the theatre (fig. 2), that of the perspective scenery beyond the main doorway (*ianua regia*) and the side ones (*hospitalia*) in the monumental facade, which is an integral part of the theatre, has been more controversial.

It has for some time been assigned by the more authoritative critics to Vincenzo Scamozzi, on the basis of the artist's own claims in a passage from his essay on the *Idea dell'architettura universale* and of the credible testimony of contemporary reports of the opening show. However, it was in the past often referred to Palladio and to

15-17. The series of photos
reconstructs the original
entrance route to the
auditorium from the peristyle

next pages:
18. Peristyle

his son Silla on the basis of specious reasoning due to a persistent anti-Scamozzi prejudice.

The arguments of those scholars convinced of Scamozzi's authorship of the scenery have recently found further confirmation in a previously ignored document. This is a passage from the draft of the *Memorie dell'Accademia* written by Pompeo Trissino, which unequivocally clarifies Palladio's responsibility and the limits of his work and the subsequent work by Scamozzi, clearly distinguishing 'the model (of the theatre) by our Palladio' from the 'perspectives ... made by Signor Vicenzo Scamocio, our compatriot, in fine and artful manner'.

The creation of the scenery, with its several focal points, and the lighting can therefore certainly be attributed to Scamozzi (1548-1616), the Vicentine architect of the generation after Palladio. But so can a whole series of completion works on the theatre decided during the important academic session of 6 May 1584, from the layout of the stage to the installation of the orchestra pit and curtain and the theatre roof. Scamozzi was the controversial inheritor of Palladio's architectural culture, an expert on perspective and theatres and an essayist, who was at the time already active on prestigious building sites.

So Scamozzi's presence on the Olimpico site began from that date, following the ineffectual interval of Silla Palladio, Andrea's son, who had taken over from him at first as works director. Scamozzi was the effective director of the finishing works to the theatre, on which he stamped the mark of his pragmatic personality and his updated and scientist knowledge.

Conceived specifically for the opening performance of Sophocles' *Oedipus the King*, 'the outstanding stage, and perspective painting',

designed by Scamozzi for the occasion but which has survived the centuries, ideally depicts the seven roads of Thebes, the location of the tragedy, but actually shows views of contemporary Vicenza: rows of 'fine blocks of flats and *palazzi*' projected towards a distant horizon using the perspective artifice of a rising floor and transformed by masterly control of the lights (fig. 21).

Considerable graphic documentation of the conception stage of the Olimpico scenery remains – four drawings in public collections (Florence, Uffizi, Gabinetto Disegni e Stampe) and one in a private collection (Chatsworth, Coll. Devonshire) (fig. 20) – showing Scamozzi's planning approach. This is quite different from Palladio's, also in terms of method.

The miraculous and unrepeatable synthesis of the Teatro Olimpico thus arose from the enforced matching of different personalities and cultures, in which two worlds and two epochs are contrasted, coming together on the plane of the proscenium (fig. 1): here the sunny, certain world of ideal models and timeless *exempla*; there the critical and doubtful one of research and tested solutions. On one hand, to say it with the charming words of Giacomo Dolfin, reporting on the opening performance, the 'hard, real, not false' architecture, of the 'wonderful order of the stage'; on the other 'the interior perspectives made by Tamoscio ...

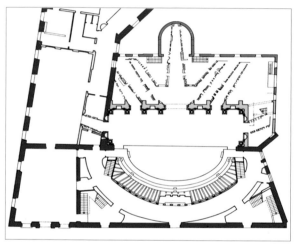

19. Layout

Key:

■
pre-existent

▨
by
Andrea Palladio

▨
by
Vincenzo Scamozzi

which are nothing when not lit, but illuminated show every detail'. Scamozzi's scenery, which called for the acquisition of an additional plot of land toward the east, went beyond Palladio's thinking on the question, which is not documented and can only be reconstructed conjecturally on the basis of the R.I.B.A. drawing (fig. 14). From this it seems fair to suppose the existence of plastic scenery of reduced size behind the white arch of the central door, though this is not indicated, replaced in the *hospitalia* by painted boards, as the different chromatic treatment of the two openings compared to the central one seems to suggest.

Theatre space as place of illusion

Although the architecture tends to surpass the scenery at the Olimpico, as also shown by the prevalent use of the building over the centuries as a professional place of entertainment rather than of dramatic performance, Palladio and Scamozzi's creation was originally conceived as a theatre space and as such mainly qualifies as a privileged place of illusion, pretence, artifice and wonder.

Everything adheres to the typical conventions of theatre buildings and stagings and is part of the spatial illusionism: the spatial simu-

lation which, on the example of the classical theatres of antiquity, transforms the closed, covered area of the old prison into an open, airy space through the amazing invention of the colonnaded exedra surmounting the cavea and the false sky above; the transformation of the modest materials used – brick, local stone, wood, stucco – into the precious appearance of marble, thanks to technical procedures of consummate experience; the perspective artifice that extends the roads of Thebes/Vicenza well beyond the actual 12 metre depth; and the pretence of the wooden scenery, as magnificent outside as it is humble and precarious inside (fig. 23).

Even the statues, pretentious portrayals of an aristocratic clientele, reveal the truth of their structure on closer observation. They are made not from stone, as they seem at first sight, but from assorted materials combined in an ingenious and expert manner: swamp reeds or tow used as insulation around an iron core that constitutes the frame, covered with layers of earthenware and mortar of a gradually finer grain, through to the surface layers in stucco, rich in gypsum to slow down the setting and simplify the moulding.

To all this is added the intangible but striking element of the light, controlled by Scamozzi's expert lighting direction, the real 'marvel' of the opening show.

The lighting units from the original stage lighting system still exist, consisting of bulbs of glass, filled for the occasion with coloured oils, or of sets of wicks set in metal boxes. They were placed in hidden parts of the false architecture; a network of light-

ing points making up the 'thousand and one invisible, hidden lights' of which Dolfin spoke 'so that only the illuminated atmosphere appeared, without it being apparent where the light came from, making men think that inside it was day, and outside obviously night'.

The statues in the Palladio hall:
'casting the academician founders of the theatre in stone'
and the question of 'everlasting memory'

The busy collection of stucco statues crowding the proscenium and wings (42 in total, now reduced to 41 due to the loss of a statue from the upper tier) and decorating the niches of the exedra (21), depicting the founder academicians and contemporary with the building of the theatre (fig. 24), play an important role in shaping the unique, inimitable physiognomy of the Olimpico.

To these are added the stone statues on the baluster above the peristyle and in the staircase niches (32), intended from the start but not made until the mid-eighteenth century, by Giacomo Cassetti. They include not only Olympians, but also people of importance such as Giangiorgio Trissino, who is positioned alongside Andrea Palladio, as shall be seen.

The decorative plan largely dates from the Palladio design that has come down to us (fig. 14), apart from the alterations of content made after Andrea's death. It conceived the plastic elements not as an ornamental addition, but as an integral part of the architectural structure, which it

previous pages:
21. Scenery perspectives

22. Scenery perspectives

23. Scenery perspectives seen from behind

helps articulate in space and emphasise in terms of chiaroscuro (figs. 24-25).

The decoration of the theatre, a critical and highly significant chapter in the history of the Accademia, may be exhaustively reconstructed through the minutes of the meetings and other acts of the association. A picture of noble passions and proud proposals clearly emerges from this, but also one of prosaic realities – differences of opinion, rivalries and defaults on the part of the members – in a mixture of 'poverty and nobility'. These were, however, fully redeemed and transformed into the definitive appearance of the theatre, consecrated by the opening performance on 3 March 1585. The question of the statues, destined with one thing and another to continue through the entire course of the works on the theatre, was opened and generally defined by late spring 1580. From the begin-

ning it reflected a clear desire for self-celebration and perpetuity on
the part of the commissioning body, which in the sitting of 23 May
of that year decided that it was 'very fitting that, making such hon-
oured investment in something eternal (the theatre), the memory
of those academicians who contributed to it should also remain
eternal'.

Originally intended as a big allegorical parade with female and
male statues of a symbolic nature, linked to the individual members only by the name shown on the base and all 'equal in terms of
cost', the decorative project was subject to difficulties and contro-
versies that moved it further and further away from the original
intentions, before coming to a historic turn, decided in the meeting
of 7 April 1582. The new direction, destined to remain unchanged
through to the end of the works, established that 'each academician
must have his statue made in the figure of a man dressed, or armed,
in antique style; his effigy may be a likeness, and those that have
already been done in the figures of females must be remade in the
form of males'.

The choice of the portrait-statue, though also functional in terms of
soliciting the increasingly begrudging contributions of members,
confirms the academicians' desire for self-celebration; they saw in
it the realisation of their aspirations to pass from the time of the
daily report to that of history.

In a singular doubling, particularly suited to the theatre, the
patrons-spectators thus reflect one another in their petrified effigies on the front of the proscenium, clasped in armour or draped in
long gowns or capes in classical style.

Although clearly restated, the question of the statues was still slow
in being translated into reality, and it was left to *Principe* Leonardo
Valmarana to imperiously take up the reins less than a year after
the opening, stipulating a contract on 9 May 1584 with the Lom-
bard sculptors Ruggero Bascapé and Domenico Fontana to ensure
the completion and alteration, where necessary, of the decorative
works already carried out on the proscenium. The clauses of the
contract included production of the missing statues, 'remaking' of
those already made in the form of women, inscriptions with members' names on the pedestals and the creation of bas-reliefs for the
third tier, of which more will be said below.

Visible signs of the operation to convert the already made female
statues into male ones, shown in the documents, remain in the
body of the monument. The statue of Gerolamo Forni, in the third
upper tier, in the corner of the left wing, has a virile, bearded head
that has been adapted to a body that is unequivocally that of a
woman, while in the nearby one of Giovan Battista Tittoni,
although the hair has been adapted, the facial features retain a
sweetness that is entirely feminine (fig. 26).

In line with the new direction and under the authoritative guide of
Valmarana, the troublesome question of the statues neared its con-

25. The statues of three academicians: Girolamo da Schio, Giovanni Filippo Banca and Pietro Capra, in the upper tier on the right

clusion, apart from the inexplicable exception of the missing inscriptions under most of the academicians' effigies.

The gallery of figures arranged on plinths and within shrines on the proscenium is extremely evocative, encouraging the spectator to identify them. This is simple enough for 11 of them, whose names are inscribed on the pedestals, but is possible for each through the Accademia documents.

Thus, with their identities restored and evoked, exponents of the old nobility of blood such as the Trissino, Chiericati, Valmarana and Thiene families, representatives of the more recent aristocracy of wealth, such as the Barbarano and Caldogno, noble figures of literati and philosophers like Anton Maria Angiolelli and Giovambattista Ghellini, illustrious doctors like Fabio Pace, artists like Girolamo Forni and others are revived, methodically arranged in the composed order of the stage and the exedra.

Defined by critics as 'the most original Vicentine, if not Italian, museum of late sixteenth-century sculpture', the statuary collection of the Olimpico is a group work, also in terms of artistry. It is to be appreciated more as a whole than for its single elements, in which there is an apparent discontinuity of style and quality, inevitably linked to the importance of the person depicted and the size of the sum paid. Despite the difficulties created by the tortuous path of history, it is still possible to distinguish the contribution of some of the more qualified and renowned sculptors and to recognise the figures of assistants, on the basis of documents and matters of style within the work.

According to an attribution supported by the initials A.R. inscribed on the pedestal, the statue of Pompeo Trissino (fig. 27) is by Agostino Rubini, nephew of the great Alessandro Vittoria and leading exponent of the Vicenza school of sculpture, who was active at the Olimpico through to 1583 when he left the city for Venice. There is an evident intent to create a likeness in this statue of the noble, son of Ciro and grandson of Giangiorgio Trissino, from the Trissino del Vello d'oro branch, in the detailed finesse of the face ending in the short, pointed beard, and the insistent attention to detail in the curly fleece of the small ram he holds in his right hand, alluding to his family name, recalling the mythical adventures of the Argonauts.

26. The statue of Giambattista Tittoni, in the left corner of the upper tier

27. The statue of Pompeo Trissino, in one of the first tier niches on the right of the proscenium

The fine statue of Leonardo Valmarana (fig. 28) at the centre of the exedra semi-circle, in line with the main door and the central road, on the other hand, is by Bascapé, according to considerations of style and confirmed by probable links between the artist and client. A descendant of one of the oldest and most notable families of the Vicentine nobility, always loyal to the Habsburg cause, Valmarana is portrayed with imperial attributes: a crown of laurel, sceptre, globe and Toson d'oro collar, and has the facial features of Charles v, the incarnation of the idea of empire.

He associated a subtle discourse of identification in self-celebratory manner to an obsequious appeal to the great deceased Spanish sovereign, aimed at presenting himself as an emulator of the emperor: he, too, being sovereign of the restricted and qualified microcosm of the academicians.

Appointed *principe* from 1583 to 1585, Valmarana left the sign of his charismatic and energetic personality on the final stage of the works, on which he played a decisive role in terms of organisation and personal financial contribution. His proud, strong-willed image, which dominates the podium of the cavea, marked the official end to the historic adventure of the Teatro Olimpico, five years after work began and exactly thirty after the foundation of the Accademia.

The reliefs with *Episodes from the Life of Heracles*: a chapter of humanist culture in euhemeristic vein

The decoration of the proscenium and wings is completed by a series of stucco bas-reliefs portraying *Episodes from the Life of Heracles* in the upper tier or attic, between the statues.

In comparison with the majestic but irregular statuary complex just examined, the bas-reliefs are the most united and certain part of the theatre's overall decorations in terms of chronology and authorship, and of overall quality.

A certain *post quem* limit for the creation of the panels is given by the already mentioned contract of 9 May 1584, which establishes that the contracting artists, Ruggero Bascapé and Domenico Fontana, were to 'make new versions of the twelve stories missing from the upper tier of the said facade'. The central bas-relief with the academic emblem, flanked by two representations of *Fame* with long trumpets extended and the two images of *Glory* crowned with laurels above the arch of the central door, are evidently also part of the overall complex.

The effective authorship of the work and the leading role of the pair of sculptors mentioned are also attested by the signature RUGER BASCAPE F., engraved on the pedestal of the circus obelisk in the central attic panel. This is an incontrovertible document that definitively invalidates all previous attributions to Agostino Rubini made by some scholars.

The cycle does not correspond to the traditional one of the twelve

IOANNI
MONTIA
LEONIS.F

Labours, but is reduced and interpreted, to adapt it to the spaces available in the architectural layout.

The episodes shown, proceeding from the outside extremity of the left wing toward the right, are: *Heracles taking Atlas' place holding up the world, Heracles overcoming the triform Geryon, Heracles overpowering Antaeus, Heracles and Deianira abducted by Nessus, Hercules killing the Nemean Lion* and, beyond the frame with the emblem and motto, *Heracles fighting the centaurs, Heracles killing Cacus with his club, Heracles killing the Cretan bull, Heracles defeating the three-headed Cerberus* and *Heracles capturing the Hydra of Lerna*. The series is completed by two episodes showing *Heracles fighting the Stymphalides* and *Heracles killing the Erymanthian boar* in small frames above the doors in the wings.

The panel with the Accademia's emblem, whose meaning was discussed above, is at the centre of the attic. It consists of the passage from Virgil and the race of chariots in the circus, alluding to the Olympic games. The complete version of the inscription, HOC OPUS HIC LABOR EST, was rediscovered during the last restoration of the theatre (1985-7), under a layer of plaster that carried the abbreviated form HOC OPUS. This alteration was probably made by the academicians before the opening of the theatre. Once the building was complete, they preferred to favour the triumphalist and celebrative moment in their motto: the *opus*, ignoring the idea of effort, the *labor*, required to achieve it, as superfluous if not unseemly.

Already considered 'stunning' by the literature of the eighteenth and nineteenth centuries, the bas-reliefs are of a surprisingly high quality and show characteristics of style that were foreign to the Vicentine artistic world of the time. They were closer, rather, to those of the Milan circle gravitating around the figure of Leone Leoni, an accredited sculptor of the Habsburg court, where Bascapé, a native of Landriano, near Pavia, may have been trained.

Bascapé, here in his first work of note, laid out the scenes of the panels according to expert compositional styles and a well-chosen narrative theme, showing complete command of the expressive media and consummate technical skill, combining a robust plastic sense with lively naturalism. It is clear that he has fully absorbed the classical lesson, but is already open to the achievements of baroque sculpture. This is evident, for example, in the scene of *Heracles overpowering Antaeus* (fig. 29), where the plastic vividness of the characters in the foreground contrasts with the pictorial nature of the backgrounds, which evoke hints of rural elements, such as the group of houses set on the hills in the shadow of a thick, masterfully depicted stand of trees.

The portrayal of the stories, marked by a lively and dynamic tone, is generally used as a pretext for displays of athletic and vigorous nudes, as in the scene of *Heracles killing Cacus with his Club* or that of *Heracles killing the Cretan Bull* (fig. 30), one of the finest in the cycle, where the din from the clash of contrasted forces, human and

30. Heracles killing
the Cretan Bull, bas-relief
on the proscenium attic

animal, is very effectively suggested by the powerful musculature of the hero in the act of checking the blind charge of the beast with his knee.

Although the theme inspired by the figure of Heracles is consistent with the dedication and title of the Accademia itself, it is clearly derived from the theories of Euhemerus, a Greek writer of the fourth-third century BC, on the nature of the gods. He considered them not as abstract entities but as illustrious men who really existed and won eternal glory through their own actions, and were thus popularly considered divine and therefore immortal.

In line with the humanist and Renaissance interpretation of Euhemerus' thinking, the myth of Heracles took on an exemplary value for the Olympians, and the bas-reliefs on the attic, charged with a precious allegorical message, stand as a metaphor for the aspirations of the commissioning body. They are thus a permanent reminder to its members to work well to win fame and glory, which are the requirements for the immortality of memory to which the Accademia aspired.

'Anno MDLXXXIIII Palladio archit[ecto]', a stone and a statue: recognition, but late and lacking sincerity

The Olimpico council voted on the decision to dedicate a statue to '*M. Andrea Palladio Accademico et architetto del Teatro con iscrizione debita alla sua virtù*' (M. Andrea Palladio, Academician and architect of the theatre with suitable inscription to his virtue) with a resolution of 24 April 1582, agreeing to position this in the third upper row, at the outside edge of the right wing. As a result of the resolution, the name of the maestro was entered at forty-second place on the general list of positions for the statues, already drawn up in April of the previous year, in the place of two names that had been deleted.

The long period that had passed since Palladio's death in August 1580 and the background position assigned to his image within the overall sculptural complex suggest that there was little conviction behind the decision and some resistance rather than convinced approval, making this more an act of duty than sincerity. Indeed, although unanimously approved, the proposal came to nothing and the image of Palladio was substituted by that of Gerolamo Porto, now missing.

In place of a statue among his aristocratic colleagues, Palladio was given a citation within the proscenium inscription, conceived by Paolo Teggia in 1584. But in this case, too, the recognition of the Olympians' debt to their great 'co-academic' was not unanimous or spontaneous but, as shown by the sources, controversial and the object of a demeaning dispute on the appropriateness of the gesture, given his non-noble social extraction. Finally agreed, the inscription was in any case limited to awarding Palladio a subordinate and solely operational role in the historic theatre project, indi-

cated by the smaller characters and the abbreviated form of the citation, compared to the real protagonists of the work: it was built, as shown in the epigraph in large letters, VIRTUTI AC GENIO OLYMPICO-RUM, that is, thanks to the merit and intelligence of the Olympians. Only around the mid-eighteenth century, in a late flicker of recognition, did the Accademia dedicate one of the mediocre statues to the designer of its theatre. This is on the peristyle baluster beside the central window, alongside that of Giangiorgio Trissino, the architect's noble patron, who had chosen for him, the son of the miller Pietro della Gondola and originally a humble stonecutter, the classical and high-sounding name of Palladio.

Alla ducale and 'false air' ceiling, or single curtain?
The terms of a raging debate

One of the problems left unresolved by the sudden death of Palladio, apart from the question of the perspectives, was that of the theatre roof, a matter the R.I.B.A. (fig. 14) drawing is not able to clarify and for which there are no precedents in Palladio's work.

The roofing solution for the stage is documented by an engraving by Ottavio Bruti Revese of 1620, so not long after completion of the theatre. It shows a wooden lacunar ceiling (*alla ducale*) enriched with stuccoes and painted areas inspired by the canonical one of classical stages, which can be credibly dated to Palladio's invention based on his knowledge of Roman theatres. There is, however, a lack of con-

temporary information or graphic documentation on how the area of the cavea was roofed, though it is plausible that it was originally covered with a curtain, in imitation of those that protected the audience from the sun and bad weather in the antique theatre buildings and that this solution had already been planned by Palladio.

31. Giovanni Picutti, drawing for the curtain, 1829

In the middle of the eighteenth century, nourished by renewed interest in Palladio's architecture precisely in that century and aroused by one of the recurring restorations of the roof and ceilings, a raging debate flared up on the question of the Olimpico roof, as conceived by its designer.

The controversy, of which traces remain in numerous publications, broke out firstly in the Accademia itself, before expanding beyond the confines of Vicenza, and saw Enea Arnaldi and Ottone Calderari taking up opposing sides. Arnaldi supported a separate solution for the *alla ducale* ceiling and for the cavea ceiling; Calderari argued for one complete roof in the form of a single curtain. The latter finally prevailed and this led to the creation of a 'curtain' stretched evenly over the stage area and that of the audience in 1829, to an elegant design by Giovanni Picutti (fig. 31). It was replaced in 1866 by a more softly draped curtain supported by a big wooden clasp at the height of the proscenium arch. This solution remained in place until the second decade of the twentieth century (1914), when Ludovico Pogliaghi repaired the *alla ducale* ceiling and once again proposed the pictorial decoration in the form of big designs originally included within the lacunae, again inspired by the figure of Heracles and representations of *Fame*.

In the same years, Federico Bialetti and Umberto Brambilla painted the false sky with white clouds over the cavea that we see today.

The theatre and its tragedy: the opening performance of Sophocles' *Oedipus the King*

The Teatro Olimpico was officially opened on 3 March 1585, the last Sunday of carnival, with a performance of *Oedipus the King* by Sophocles, an event that had a resounding effect in the papers and in history, in Italy and abroad, and quickly became part of international culture.

The choice of the play, made after long debate, appropriately linked the new, classically-inspired theatre to the classical tragedy *par excellence*, indicated as exemplary by Aristotle himself in his *Poetics*. In 1579, at the time of voting to resume theatre performances, the academicians had planned to stage a pastoral tale for the subsequent carnival of 1580, initially identified as *Euqenio* by Fabio Pace, but this was temporarily set aside because of the decision to build a permanent theatre.

The question of the performance had then been neglected during the first two years of construction, but took on importance again in 1583, a year the documents show was dominated by the drama debate, at first centred on the alternative between a pastoral, an enjoyable genre much in vogue, or a tragedy.

Various works were proposed – many composed by the academicians themselves – and rejected, until the idea of Sophocles' *Oedipus Rex*, in the version by the Venetian noble Orsatto Giustiniani, finally prevailed as the play most suited to the dignity of the place and to the Olympians' cultural project, as well as being dense with political allusions, which they relished.

The play having been chosen, by 1584 the operational stage was finally launched, under the willing and capable direction of *Principe* Valmarana, as shown by the important academic sitting of 6 May in which all the technical and organisational aspects of the opening show the following year were quickly and clearly decided. The staging of 3 March 1585, so carefully prepared, thus proved to be a memorable masterpiece, thanks also to the exceptional cast.

The play was directed by Angelo Ingegneri, an eclectic Venetian noble, Olimpico member since April 1580 and involved from the start of the theatre project, assisted by Scamozzi on the perspective scenery and lighting.

The choir master was the celebrated organist from St Mark's ducal chapel, Andrea Gabrieli, who produced his final work for the Vicenza show.

Documents show that there were important figures from the theatre world among the actors, such as the well-known Groto, called il Cieco di Adria, who took the part of Oedipus, and Giovan Battista Verato and his daughter, in the roles of Tiresias and Jocasta; the highly acclaimed Isabetta and Lucietta Pellizzari appeared among the musician-singers.

The opulent and magnificently coloured costumes were designed by the poet-painter Giovan Battista Maganza, called Magagnò; the preparatory models are still extant in public and private foreign collections.

32. Damaged statue of Heracles, patron of the Accademia, in the odeum

next pages:
33. The odeum

A large number of people came from the neighbouring cities, stretching the theatre's organisational arrangements and reception facilities. Although the exaggerated figure of 3,000 people reported by Filippo Pigafetta was not reached, the audience for this memorable evening was estimated at around 1,500.

They began arriving in the early hours of the morning and stayed until evening, 'possibly eleven hours, without any regrets at all', as Pigafetta recalls, distracted as they were by the social encounters and cheered up by the refreshments with 'wine and fruit'. Finally, when the curtain went up, an 'immense pleasure' was felt by the audience at the sight of the grandiose proscenium and the illuminated perspectives, while a 'very sweet scent of perfumes' and 'far-off harmonised music of voices and instruments' pervaded the atmosphere.

The extraordinary success sealed the use of the theatre for the future, linking it more or less irrevocably to the opening performance, as the only possible show in that classically shaped space.

Vestibule and odeum

The northern side of the theatre houses the vestibule and odeum, intended for reception and entertainment purposes by the Accademia, which help to underscore the monumental and solemn nature of the theatre.

Pompeo Trissino was responsible for the decoration of the former and the construction of the latter in the period between 1596 and 1608, during which the nobleman repeatedly held the office of *principe* of the association.

The vestibule is connected to the outside by the doorway onto Stradella del Teatro, the historic entrance to the complex. Its upper walls are decorated with a frieze of monochrome panels portraying 'the most noble actions of the Accademia'. Painted in 1596 by Alessandro Maganza, these frescoes represent, in clockwise direction and chronological order, the previously mentioned performances of *L'amor costante* and *Sofonisba*, the opening performance of *Oedipus*, a weapons tournament, the Accademia's emblem with the abbreviated motto HOC OPUS and the diplomatic mission of Japanese envoys. The decoration of the room should have been completed, according to the sources and the most recent studies, by a gallery of emblems – mottos and portrayals – referring to Accademia members, constituting an interesting iconological programme, now lost.

The adjacent odeum was built by Scamozzi in 1608 by knocking down previous partitioning to give a greater size and dignity of proportion to the room, under the new direction of Trissino. This is noted in the inscription above the connecting door to the vestibule, which carries the names of the Olympians who supported and generously contributed to its erection.

The frescoes decorating its walls, consisting of 28 monochrome figures in yellow earth, date from a few decades later (1647-8). The quality of these is difficult to judge due to their state of decay, but they are attributed to Francesco Maffei (1605-60), possibly with assistants. They represent *Olympic Divinities in niches* in the lower section, supposedly identified with personifications of the planets, and *Allegorical Portrayals of the Months and the Corresponding Signs of the Zodiac* in the upper part, alternating with spaces for the commemorative plaques. They make up a cycle still in sixteenth-century style, inspired by the search for natural truths that was dear to the Olympians. Sections of unfinished decoration also survive alongside the main figures showing the emblems of the academicians.

Photolithograph
Fotolito Veneta, San Martino Buonalbergo (Verona)

CTP printing plates and colour separations
Linotipia Saccuman s.r.l., Vicenza

Printed by
La Grafica & Stampa s.r.l., Vicenza
for Marsilio Editori® s.p.a., Venice

EDITION   YEAR

10 9 8 7 6 5 4   2010 2011 2012 2013 2014